METAVERSE

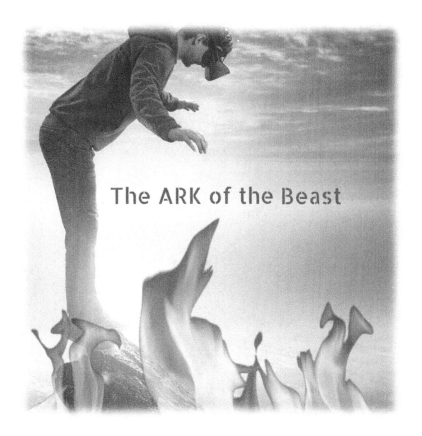

The ARK of the Beast

Dr. June Dawn Knight

Dr. June Dawn Knight

Treehouse Publishers
www.treehousepublishers.com
Printed in the United States of America

DEDICATION

Thank you to all of my supporters and family who chat while I'm live. I love the flowers, gifts, support, prayers, love that you give me. Thank you for partnering with me while I obey the Lord. Thus, I am dedicating this book to the TRUE BRIDE. You guys are amazing! You are researchers and I know God just smiles on you all. Love love love you!

METAVERSE – The Ark of the Beast

@2022 Dr. June Dawn Knight

5th Book in the *What the World?* Series

CONTENTS

I actually captured this float with London 2012 all over it!

1
Metaverse as the Ark?

The Bible says in the last days that it will be **as in the days of Noah**.

Matthew 24:^{37} But as the days of Noah were, so shall also the coming of the Son of man be

---

We have been studying the Book of Genesis this winter (2022), with a fresh lens based upon our understanding of the end of days. It is the most amazing thing now to see how God put all of this together and then see how Lucifer is doing the direct opposite. Each study brings out more revelation.

I had a revelation the other day during my Bible Study on Genesis Chapter 6. Look at this artwork:

In Genesis Chapter 6, we discovered what God meant by the judgment to Noah's generation.

We discovered that the angels had sex with the humans and created hybrids. This means that they mixed species.

Due to the mixing of entities, God's punishment was released. They were damned from that point. The angels came unto God's natural creation. Due to this mixing, life changed in the Earth such as violence increased and evil imaginations. Basically, no soul.

Thus, God released his first judgment by reducing their time on the Earth. They previously lived up to 1,000 years. Now they only live up to 120 years. This really upset God when He saw how deprived mankind became. God hates mixing.

4 There were giants in the earth in those days; and also after that, when the sons of God came in unto the daughters of men, and they bare children to them, the same became mighty men which were of old, men of renown.

We see here that the humans bear children unto these angels are created hybrid beings. This is a mixture of true natural DNA. You can only assume that when there are hybrid creations that the spirit of God is not there. They are unholy and do not carry the breath or the DNA ID of God.

There are many who believe that Eve, when she ate of the fruit had sex with Satan and begot a hybrid – Cain. They call it the Serpent Seed doctrine. They believe that the first real human child was Seth – which led to the genealogy of Noah and Jesus. I don't understand that belief or believe it myself. However, I can see why they would even consider it because of what happened here with Noah and the angels, which led to children.

5 And God saw that the wickedness of man was great in the earth, and that every imagination of the thoughts of his heart was only evil continually.

So, we compare the Old Noah to the New Noah generation. In the days of Old Noah, when the angels mixed with the humans, it was not natural.

The angels corrupted the DNA of the humans when they inter-bred. In the Old Noah scenario, the intermingling of the species was a final separation from God. It was a dividing line.

6 And it repented the Lord that he had made man on the earth, and it grieved him at his heart.

When you say God grieved and repented, I picture this as Him crying and very sorry for what He did. The new species had built a community based upon their sin.

7 And the Lord said, I will destroy man whom I have created from the face of the earth; both man, and beast, and the creeping thing, and the fowls of the air; for it repenteth me that I have made them.

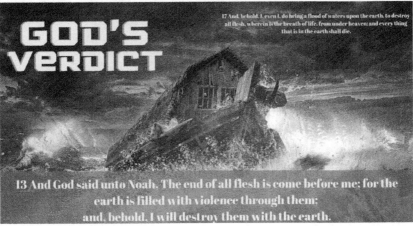

GOD'S VERDICT

17 And, behold, I, even I, do bring a flood of waters upon the earth, to destroy all flesh, wherein is the breath of life, from under heaven; and every thing that is in the earth shall die.

13 And God said unto Noah, The end of all flesh is come before me; for the earth is filled with violence through them; and, behold, I will destroy them with the earth.

8 But Noah found grace in the eyes of the Lord.

Signs of Judgment

11 The earth also was corrupt before God

and the earth was filled with violence.

Mixed with Humans and Angels
Nephilim/Hybrids

12 - FOR ALL FLESH HAD CORRUPTED HIS WAY UPON THE EARTH

22 Thus did Noah; according to all that God commanded him, so did he.

18 But with thee will I establish my covenant; and thou shalt come into the ark, thou, and thy sons, and thy wife, and thy sons' wives with thee.
19 And of every living thing of all flesh, two of every sort shalt thou bring into the ark, to keep them alive with thee; they shall be male and female.

Bringing salvation to his entire family!

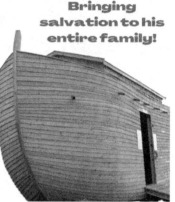

Noah obeyed God amidst all of the persecution from the people back in those days.

OLD NOAH VS. NEW NOAH (CH7)

When comparing the Old Noah versus the New Noah we must consider the commonalities of both days:

- Violence in the land
- Perversion running rampant
- Mixing of the species
- People living on the Earth as if no judgment was happening
- The mocking of Noah when warning them of pending judgment
- The evil everywhere

As we began to read Genesis Chapter 7, we discover that God saved Noah because he was righteous. This means that Noah lived a right life before God. It also meant that Noah had favor in God's eyes. He also kept himself natural and did not breed with another species. It also meant that he did not conform to the masses when they were all being angry and violent.

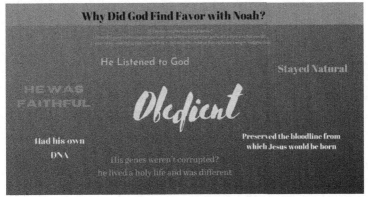

The Bride who was on this broadcast with me helped me to do these designs. We are a team. Thank you Bride!

Did you know God wanted seven of the clean beasts and two of the unclean? I thought it was just two period. It's amazing what we learned.

Then we learned that God wanted to keep the reproductive life through seeds open. Now we see how Satan is stealing that.

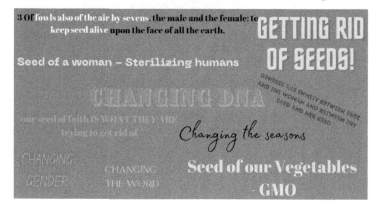

Amazing!

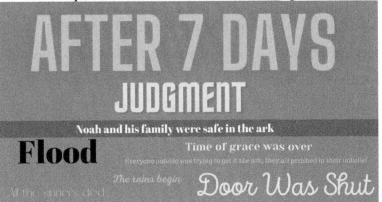

NOAH'S 7 DAY ASSIGNMENT

#7   LOAD THE ARK

1. God created the Earth in 7 days
2. God chose the clean animals by 7's
3. The rainbow by God has 7 colors
4. Seven days in a week
5. 7th Day is Sabbath
6. 7 means Completion/Rest

7 is a special number to God. Means completion.

AFTER 7 DAYS

JUDGMENT

Noah and his family were safe in the ark

Flood   Time of grace was over

Everyone outside was trying to get it the ark, they all perished in their unbelief

The rains begin   *Door Was Shut*

All the sinners died

When God shuts the door, it's a very sad day. Judgment is a very serious thing. Can you imagine those people outside the ark screaming and clawing on the door to get in and be saved from the flood? Can you imagine the anger and fear in the people as giants are in the Earth and probably battling them. They heartd Noah's warning. They mocked him. They did not see the judgment right in front of their face. Then when the door shut, there was no more grace for them. Sad.

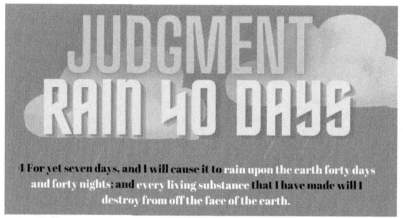

We discusses whether the naturalness of God was being destroyed by these angels because God cried and it flooded? Or maybe that God's anger brought the flood? Either way, the Earth destroyed itself. In the end because we breed with fallen angels through sex with technology (transhuman), God will destroy the Earth through fire).

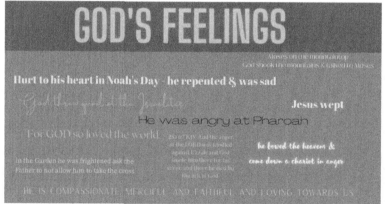

We gave many examples of God's feelings. One lady wrote me the next day and said that during her prayer that morning, God reminded her of another time he was emotional was in the Garden of Gethsemine. Jesus was begging God to take the cup. Jesus had to be emotional in the Garden. He knew His time had come.

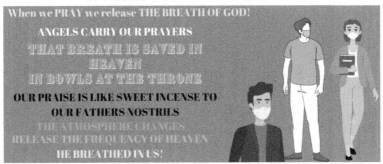

We talked about what God does when He judges. I did a study on this when I wrote the book, The American Judgment, and discovered that when God hears, smells or sees, He will act. Then we talked about two scenarios. One is when the angel comes in mid-point of Tribulation to get the saints, that it is at that time that the angels bring the bowls of our prayers from the alter and brings them to God in His temple. God smells the prayers of the Saints and He pours out His wrath in anger. He goes in His temple and tells them not to get Him until it's over! Another example was David. God saw and bowed the Heavens to help David.

Obedience is better than sacrifice.

DAYS OF NOAH

GOD - ARK	LUCIFER - METAVERSE
• Natural	• Synthetic - Fake - False
• God's creation	• Lucifer's creation - fallen angels
• God's seed	• Lucifer's seed (V)
• Future of humanity/species	• BBB OF THE SPECIES
• Preservation of DNA	• Destruction of DNA - God's naturalness
• Judgment	• Lawless abounds
• Protection of his saints	• Takes you into another world/portal
	• World of Lucifer's Playground - THE BEAST WORLD

When God told Noah to build an ark, it was all from the Earth. He told him to use wood, etc. The Ark was built for the safety and preservation of God's creation. Then we see that God created life from that ark. God preserved seed. He also killed the sinners who were not worthy to enter in.

Then when you consider Lucifer's ark, the Metaverse, then you must consider this:

- He creates a fake world to look like the real world
- Noone has flaws in this world. Noone is ugly, sick or lame
- They can access this and be a part of the world by participating in the seed.
- The MV is a trap to take the mind
- They want this world to be better than the real world because Lucifer and fallen angels created it so each human's imagination can run wild!
- It is a portal into the Beast World

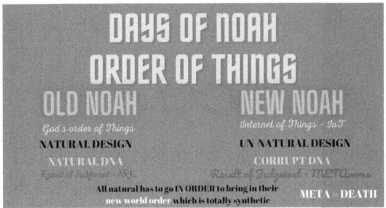

In the Old Noah day, it was natural. The supernatural came down and entered into humanity to breed and create giants. In the New Noah day, we go into Satan's world and become one with the Beast.

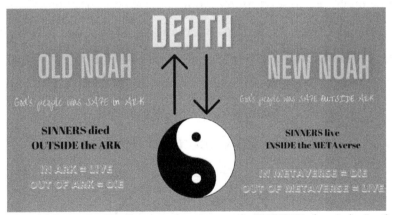

In the Old Noah, God's people were safe INSIDE the Ark. In the New Noah God's people are safe OUSIDE Lucifer's Ark.

In the Ark today we die.
Out of the Ark today we live.

In the Metaverse we die.
Out of the Metaverse we live.

We cannot give them our brain.

THE INTERSECTION OF THE CIRCLE

Today is Sunday, February 13th. The Lord gave me instructions in a dream this morning that **the key to the Metaverse is in the intersection of the two circles**. In my dream I saw a chip:

When it comes to the infinity circle, I think about the logo from the International Courts of Justice. International Courts are all over the world. I believe these will be the courts that will carry out the Noahide Laws.

(Notice the center of the circles)

International Courts of Justice Logo

Look at the show 100's logo:

International courts are over the world

- ICJ all over the world
- Sun worship
- The rising sun
- Mason bricks
- One world ruler
- Woman ruler holding scales
- Woman holding wheat
- Queen of Heaven?
- New Age where Noahide is Justice
- Lady is holding the wheat and Justice is in other hand could mean famine
- Seven (7) bricks (Noahide Laws)
- Two (2) worlds connected by a tree in the shape of a triangle
- Infinity Symbol
- Tree holding up two worlds
- Wheel within a Wheel
- As above so below?
- Brain waves like Trump's Operation Warp Speed logo
  *the tree holding up the new and old world is either the Kabbalah tree or an olive tree representing the "one world peace"

BACK TO THE INTERSECTION OF THE CIRCLE

In the next chapter, you will see the display at the London Transportation Museum from my 2012 study-abroad class. It shows how the computer chip will be key to this new world. **The world they are describing IS THE METAVERSE!** The chip is how it is all connected!

Facts you must know:

- AI is the brain to the beast - ran by the World Economic Forum. This is why the powers-that-be have made science their god. Artificial Intelligence is the god. Data runs the world and think of it like a spider.
  - The big head makes the AI
  - The body of it is the data gathered after sucking the info from the humans
  - The legs are the data being released from it to all areas involved

Let me draw a picture of what I see in the spirit…..

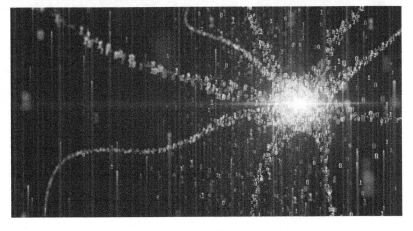

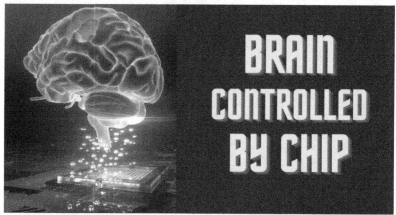

BRAIN CONTROLLED BY CHIP

HIVE MIND

hive mind

1. a notional entity consisting of a large number of people who share their knowledge or opinions with one another, regarded as producing either uncritical conformity or collective intelligence.
2. "he has become one of those celebrities whose online presence has made him a favorite of the internet hive mind"
   ◦ (in science fiction) a unified consciousness or intelligence formed by a number of alien individuals, the resulting consciousness typically exerting control over its constituent members.
   ◦ "there is a Borg Queen who controls the hive mind"

Hive Mind

- a notional entity consisting of a large number of people who share their knowledge or opinions with one another, regarded as producing either uncritical conformity or collective intelligence.
- "he has become one of those celebrities whose online presence has made him a favorite of the internet hive mind"
  - (in science fiction) a unified consciousness or intelligence formed by a number of alien individuals, the resulting consciousness typically exerting control over its constituent members.
  - "there is a Borg Queen who controls the hive mind"

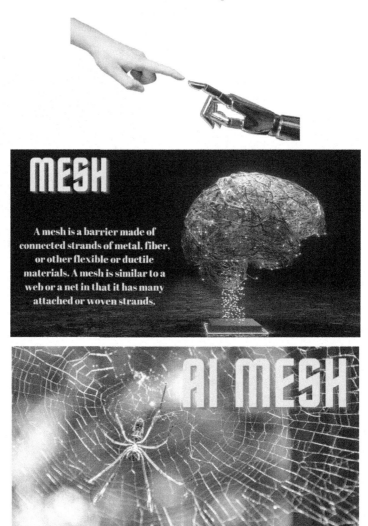

These pictures show you what I see in the spirit. Satan has a mesh prepared – an evil spider web to trap the humans. He's after the mind.

- United Nations – UN – is the body of the Beast
- World Economic Forum – AI – is the brain
- Lucifer's Eyes – Internet – Fake World

- US Capital is the belly of the beast

- White House is the mouth

- Secretary of State is the arms

- The Noahide Laws is the heart of the beast

- False prophets is the lungs

- Loins – Perversion – LGBTQ

- Legs – 5G and power booster

- Feet – Causes beast to move – media

Going back to the intersection of the circle. **The human is at the center of the circular economy**.

According to the World Economic Forum, this is how they describe this, "**Because data comes from people and is destined for people**, a relationship of trust is primordial between those that extract and collect data, those who manage and interpret it, and those who use it for ends that are either glorious or nefarious. This trust – like any other kind of relationship – can be strengthened by transparency, predictability, and slow and steady building up of bonds. The more sensitive the data, the more it is essential to move slowly, to reveal not just one's activities but also one's goals, and to invite participation and feedback from the various stakeholders."[1]

Through the lens of human-centered design, information needs, creation and distribution systems can be seen as fluid systems that adapt and regenerate according to the obstacles, challenges and needs of a given situation and community.

Combining macro-level analysis (i.e. media landscape, information infrastructures, and political/regulatory environments), granular observations (i.e. information availability, needs, and distribution), with human and social insights (i.e. identifying information disseminators and influencers) can be viewed as an important way for policymakers and practitioners to design the most appropriate and effective strategies for individuals, communities and societies.[2]

■■■

---

[1] https://www.weforum.org/agenda/2021/08/12-ways-a-human-centric-approach-to-data-can-improve-the-world/

[2] https://reports.weforum.org/data-driven-development/the-role-of-communities-and-the-individual-digital-identity-and-human-centred-design/?doing_wp_cron=1644803058.8998720645904541015625

Robotics and artificial intelligence in particular are likely to create substantial new disruption to labour markets, testing social cohesion still further. There is an urgent need for a bold policy agenda to confront this challenge combined with a visionary narrative about the improvements in everyday life that the Fourth Industrial Revolution can bring to households, countries and humanity at large. This will be no easy task, but there are specific steps that can be taken to build a different kind of economy, one with social inclusion consciously "designed into" its core.[3]

∙∙∙

US research requires reconfiguring to value the contributions of both bioscience and social and behavioral science to inform SARS-CoV-2 vaccine development. If embedded within the COVID-19 response, rapid social, behavioral, and communication science can deliver timely data and empirically based advice to support vaccine delivery strategies and uptake. In the SARS-CoV-2 vaccine enterprise, communities can be active research partners, rather than passive study subjects. Finally, human-centered design principles (aka "design thinking") can help improve the planning and implementation of the COVID-19 vaccination program.[4]

∙∙∙

In the above quotes, it provides a broad picture of the human-centered design. They are gathering data from the human and designing the world around it.

---

[3] https://www.weforum.org/agenda/2017/06/toward-a-human-centered-model-of-economic-growth/

[4] https://www.centerforhealthsecurity.org/our-work/pubs_archive/pubs-pdfs/2020/200709-The-Publics-Role-in-COVID-19-Vaccination.pdf

This is one of the reasons I've advised people to **not join Trump's Truth social media**.

It will be a bunch of angry birds talking about their anger towards what is going on (which is a setup with all of them working together).

Circular Economy

Earlier I explained how the circles intersecting each other are representative of the Circular Economy. This economy is reincarnation. Let me give you some examples:

The flagship facility, expected to open in Seattle in spring 2021, is designed to reconnect human death rituals with nature and to offer a more sustainable alternative to conventional burial options. Today, burial often involves chemical-laden embalming, while cremation uses eight times more energy, according to the architects at Olson Kundig who designed the new facility. Recompose will offer a first-of-its-kind "natural organic reduction" service on-site, which will "convert human remains into soil in about 30 days, helping nourish new life after death."[5]

Let's Look at Ikea's sustainable plan:

Designing for a circular future

Circularity is about transforming the existing 'take, make, waste' linear model to the opposite – reuse, refurbish, remanufacture, and recycle.

---

[5] https://www.fastcompany.com/90434525/the-worlds-first-human-composting-facility-could-help-us-recycle-ourselves

One key piece of the puzzle is to adopt circular thinking during the design phase of the product, developing it right from the beginning so it can reach its full circularity potential one day.

IKEA is committed to becoming a circular business by 2030. This is a great challenge and an opportunity to reshape how we see value in the things around us.[6]

••

So, as you can see, it's sort of like recycling or reincarnation. With the infinity symbol, I see it as the world of humans colliding with world of the Beast. I see it as an intersection of two species again like in the Days of Noah. The chip is the middle connector to both sides.

I hope I'm explaining this well. Look what I saw on the Superbowl today –

Notice behind the man the drones were doing the swirl in the sky, then they formed this figure (looks like sun – remember above).

Then this…

Jentzen Franklin's new church that looks like a spider. They both look like the Vatican – the snake and the spider there.

According to this article, they create buildings like this to withstand weather catastrophes. "The spiderweb style allows for high-quality sound insulation: the web absorbs or lessens the overflow of sound waves. Thanks to this observation, scientists have created materials known as "metamaterials", which, when produced in large quantities, allow the sound insulation of homes to be improved.

Frei Otto and Spiderweb Buildings

Frei Otto is a German architect, who was the first to create biometric constructions mimicking the structure of a spiderweb. According to him, our current society is looking for a return to lightness, energy efficiency and adaptability. Increasing the number of more natural constructions is very important for him. For Frei Otto, this increase would be possible with a rise in the number of spiderweb-based buildings. [7]

This also reminds me of how they are doing the infrastructure preparing for terrible weather. The poles are very thick metal poles, etc. Wonder what they know that we don't know?

Conclusion

Hopefully you can see the comparison of the Old Noah versus the New Noah. We are here at this time. The hybrids are happening now through Crispr program. They are mixing iron with clay, human blood with animals, plants and other species. We also see the signs of the violence in the land, perversion and the obvious blinding of people when it comes to the hour we are living in.

---

[7] https://www.find-my-architect.com/uk/en/actualite/buildings-based-on-spider-webs#:~:text=The%20shape%20of%20a%20spiderweb,to%20replace%20the%20spider's%20fibre.&text=This%20type%20of%20structure%2C%20like,those%20with%20a%20traditional%20frame.

2
Keys from London

When I was in London in 2012, the Lord revealed to me the human implantation chip and the connection of the Internet of Things – IoT. This chip is the mark of the beast. I wrote my college paper on this in graduate school and made a grade of 100. This became my first book, *Mark of the Beast.*

I inserted some of my pictures when I was in London in a couple of these WTW books.

When I was in London in 2011/2012 winter Study-Abroad classes with the University of Kentucky, I visited the London Transportation Museum one day and discovered the plan of the Beast. This was divine appointment! I was not living right and did not want to see this, but when I did, my mouth fell to the floor. I knew the end had already arrived! The days I feared since I was a kid.

I feel like God revealed this to me while I was there. Who would have known that **seven years later I would be in the White House witnessing this plan come to fruition**? Pretty crazy huh? You can't make this stuff up! LOL.

I am standing on the Meridian Line 2012.

The meridian line in Greenwich represents the Prime Meridian of the world, Longitude Zero (0° 0' 0"). Every place on the Earth is measured in terms of its angle east or west from this line.

Since 1884, the Prime Meridian has served as the reference point for Greenwich Mean Time (GMT). The line runs across the courtyard of the Royal Observatory and was adopted by international agreement to the irritation of the French who continued to use the Paris meridian.[8]

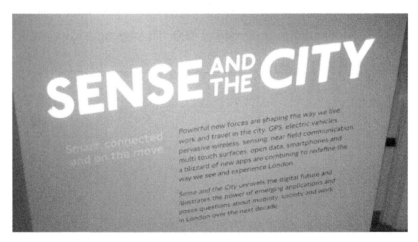

This was the exhibit. I still have the pictures. In this exhibit, notice how they say "open data". This is the normalization taking place now with the merging of the countries, businesses, medical field, religion and governments. This process is how the Internet of Things (IoT) is built. It is combining everything through AI – artificial intelligence. This is the SMART world. SMART devices. Everything talks to one another through data nodes, etc.

---

[8] https://www.royalparks.org.uk/parks/greenwich-park/things-to-see-and-do/the-meridian-line

This is why they say "equity" – it's because there will be no excuses. It's all by the law of the computer (AI).

In this exhibit I learned about the human implantation chip. They displayed it in the center of the room (I have a picture of this as well). Now I know why they did that. **In the circular economy, the human is at the center of everything.**

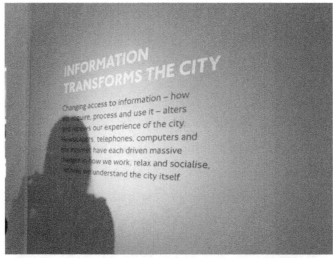

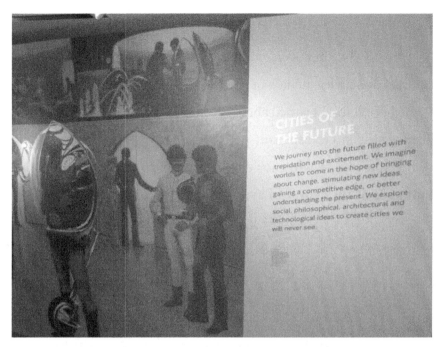

These cities they are talking about are SMART cities that are being built now.

120 years ago

Telephones become indispensable for businesses, but all calls must be routed by a human switchboard operator. Initially, only used for serious conversations. Switchboard operators interrupt any conversation they considered too frivolous.

63 years ago

Full automation of the UK telephone network begins. By 1978 you can call anywhere in the UK without going through a human operator.

26 years ago

Two Vodafone employees make the first mobile phone call in the UK. New generations of phones follow adding text messaging in 1991 and Internet access in 2000.

This picture shows how shopping has changed over the years. Notice how it says you can shop without cash. This is from 2012.

2100 years ago

The first coins in Britain minted by the Celtic tribes. We have to wait until 1694 for the Bank of England to issue the first banknotes. Over the years, watermarks, metal threads, holograms and ultra-violet printing are added to prove authenticity and to prevent forgeries.

45 years ago

Barclaycard launched the first credit card in the UK. A magnetic strip on the back holds account information period from 2004, UK credit cards contain a data chip which must be verified with the holders PIN.

16 years ago

Ebay founded a computer programmer, Pierre Omidyar. A trusted digital payment method is essential to eBay success, so it acquires PayPal in 2002. Today there are over 10 million items for sale on the UK site at any one time.

3 years ago

Barclaycard produces a contactless payment terminal enabling fast transactions for items worth $15 or less. A contactless payment card is held close to the reader. And the amount is deducted from the customer's account without the need for a PIN. Could this be the start of a cashless society?

This was at the bottom of the display window. Notice how they are preparing the viewers for a cashless society. This all flows together with the metaverse.

300 years ago

Newspapers proliferate as the government relaxes controls and duties on printing and paper. Hundreds of newspapers end up covering news from all points of view.

75 years ago

Millions tune in nightly during the momentous events of the mid 20th century. From the 1960s, portable transistor radios take radio out of the home.

25 years ago

The Sony Watchman is an early attempt to provide rich media on the move. Television has taken over from radio as the main source of news for most people decades ago but lacks the portability of transistor radios.

76 years ago

Penguin paper bags are published for the first time period these light-weight easy to carry books prove instantly popular and satisfy readers desire to enjoy good books anywhere anytime.

25 years ago

Atari 2600 video games console proves massively popular during the 1980s. Bringing arcade style digital entertainment into your living room period

15 years ago

Nintendo Gameboy provides digital gaming on the move as long as the AA batteries last out in these days before the integral rechargeable Power Pack.

300 years ago

Coffee houses become popular across London serving the exotic new drink. They become centres for philosophical, political and artistic debates well as venues for doing business. Lloyd's of London the insurance company was founded in Lloyd's coffee shop.

55 years ago

Italian coffee bars are the essential place for teenagers to hang out in the 1950s and 1960s providing juke box music and a hip. European vibe.

35 years ago

TimeOut is the essential guide to London listing at various times music, theater, dance, cinema, sport bars, cafes, restaurants and "agit prop" – agitation and propaganda.

7 years ago

Mark Zuckerberg founds Facebook at Harvard University. Within 5 years Facebook moves off campus to become the most popular social networking site on the planet. Users meet, chat, flirt, and also set up groups for specialist interests, political campaigns and products.

120 years ago

Morse code keys send information as the dots and dashes down Telegraph cables that encircle the world creating the Victorian Internet. Information including war news and stock prices takes just minutes to reach London from around the globe.

90 years ago

Canisters carrying documents are moved using air pressure through 120 kilometres of tubes under London. Pneumatic tube systems continue into the 21st century carrying documents, cash, medical samples and components.

Around 45 years ago

Type balls are the printing threads ofsome teletype machines forming part of the tail lakes network enabling organizations to send information electronically around the world.

35 years ago

Acoustically coupled modern connect computers over telephone lines to access bulletin boards, forerunners of Internet forums. During the 1980s, companies lay fiber optic cables, increasing the capacity of the telephone network in preparation for digital services.

40 years ago

5 inch disc begin to replace punched tape for storing digital information. Five and a half and three and a half inch disc up here in the 1970s and 80s with optical disc in the 1990s and 2000s. A USB stick can hold more data than 8billion kilometers of punched tape.

35 years ago

Program programmable calculators are cheap and small enough that people can buy their own personal piece of computing equipment. No games though.

25 years ago

The Commodore 64 computer becomes the world's best selling personal computer of all time period a record it continues holds into the 21st century. For many people the Commodore 64 is the first computer they have at home

25 years ago

The ZX spectrum enters many British homes as a competitor to EU S Commodore 64. The UK computer software industry establish is itself to fulfill demand for games and other programs

NOTICE the writing on back on picture. It states, "Evolving technologies enable increasing numbers of us to record our sense of the city while CCTV records us all."

55 years ago

Brian E cameras have transformed the photography from and expensive technologicalart form and turned it into a medium almost anyone can afford.

35 years ago

Polaroid cameras herald instant image making period film is no longer sent to laboratories for processing and amateur photographers make full use of this new privacy.

15 years ago

CCTV cameras make Britains allegedly the most watched people on the planet. Raising questions about this relative benefits of large scale surveillance.

80 years ago

Diaries have changed from narrative records of the past two list of appointments to be kept in the future

120 years ago

Two kids become a ubiquitous necessity for travel on the London bus and growing underground rail networks. Paper tickets declined with the introduction of the Oyster card for contactless payment in 2003.

120 years ago

Timetables are essential for running the railway system and ensure that the time is precisely the same across the city.

75 years ago

A to Z maps redefine how Londoners think of their city. For the first time it is easy to find addresses in neighborhood you don't know.

120 years ago

Pocket watches are carried by the most business people to show to ensure that they are on time around the city. Cheap digital watches hit the market in the 1980s. Giving everyone access to split second accuracy.

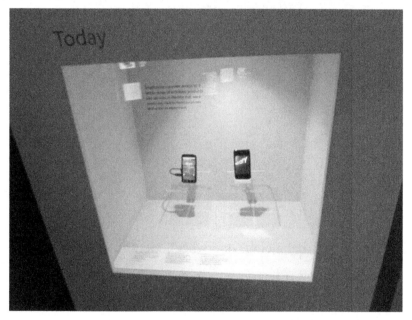

- Voice, video, email and messenger conversations anywhere
- Photography and video capture and upload with location information attached instantly
- Video downloads
- Shared diaries on the go

- Payments made through PayPal and credit card reader apps
- Barcoded picture message tickets
- Route planning, timetable and live travel information apps
- Individual and communal games
- Streamed or saved music
- 24/7 access to billions of people and millions of special interests through hundreds of social networks
- Instant location information

The RYNO self-balancing, one wheel, electric scooter aims to ease city commuting. Electric power makes it less polluting than other vehicles, while its small size means it can travel where larger vehicles cannot. www.rynomotors.wordpress.com.

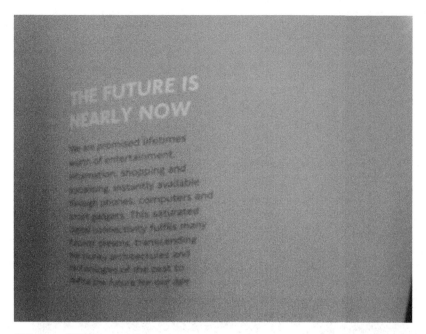

"Future" UN word.

15 years ago

Luc Besson's film *The Fifth Element* features a towering, vertiginous future city with the classic futuristic motif of the flying car.

Source: Columbia / Tri-Star /The Kobal Collection. 1997

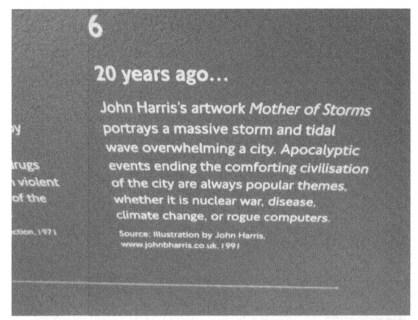

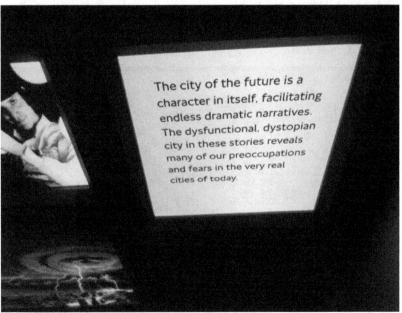

EXPANDING DIGITAL LANGUAGE

More than 14 new words appear in the English Language every day.

This wall endeavours to explain some words and phrases that have recently come into common usage in the mushrooming field of digital technology.

In June 2009, web 2.0 became the millionth English word.

Source: Global Language Monitor

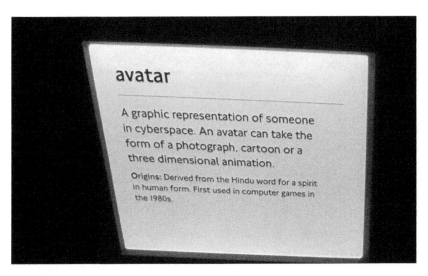

I could write a whole book on this! Look at the new TV show – *Alter Ego*. This is the digital twin of a human! Terrible!

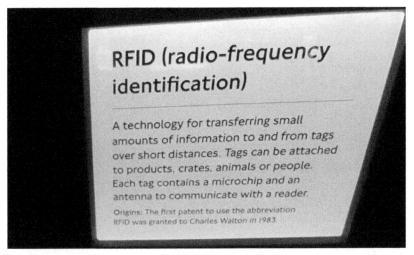

This is where I learned about the human implantation chip! I wrote my college paper on this! A few years later God told me to convert it to a book! Now look what God has done! From London to the White House! WOW!

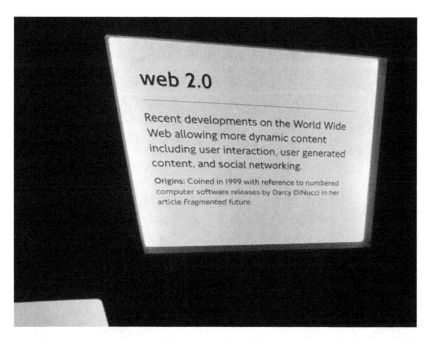

This is great way to show you the history of the internet without me having to write a whole chapter on this. These pictures spell it out!

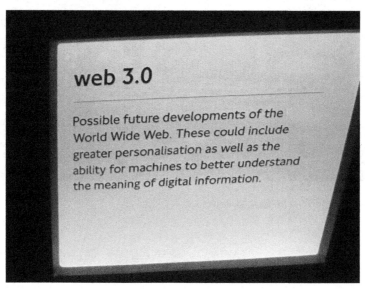

Notice the date! 2020!

What started in 2020? The Peace Deal which kicked off Tribulation! Corona starts! Wow!

This is how I learned about the **Internet of Things (IoT).** It says, "is about giving every physical object a representation in the digital world. This may be done by attaching radio communications to each object, such as RFID tags, or by attaching QR & bar codes. The IoT is providing increasing volumes of environmental and position data as well as interactivity and autonomous action for a diverse range of products, devices, vehicles

51

and buildings.

The RFID tags are inserted in the vaccines. Artificial Intelligence (AI).

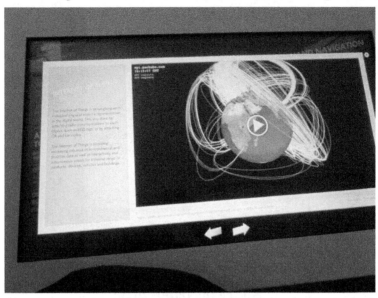

This was a video we could watch. I learned so much during this exhibit!

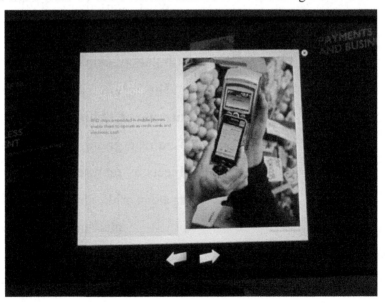

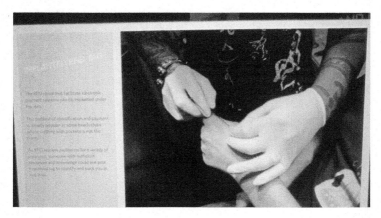

This states:

The RFID chips that facilitate electronic payment systems can be implanted under the skin.

This method of identification and payment is already popular at some beach clubs where clothing with pockets is not the norm.

As RFID readers proliferate for a variety of purposes, someone with sufficient resources and knowledge could use your implanted tag to **identify and track you in real time.**

REPEAT

As RFID readers proliferate for a variety of purposes, someone with sufficient resources and knowledge could use your implanted tag to identify and track you in real time.

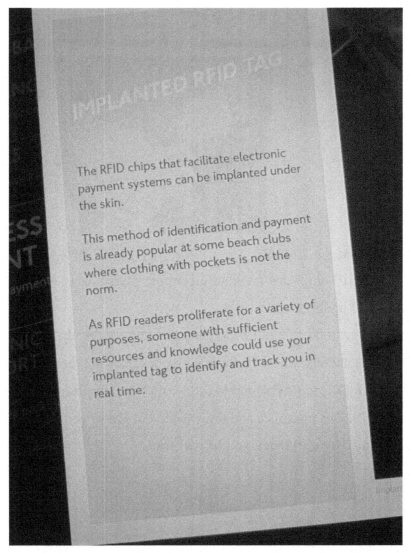

The RFID chips that facilitate electronic payment systems can be implanted under the skin.

This method of identification and payment is already popular at some beach clubs where clothing with pockets is not the norm.

As RFID readers proliferate for a variety of purposes, someone with sufficient resources and knowledge could use your implanted tag to identify and track you in real time.

In my book about CRYPTO, I will discussing how the vaccine and crypto work together. The RFID will be managing all of your data – to include banking information.

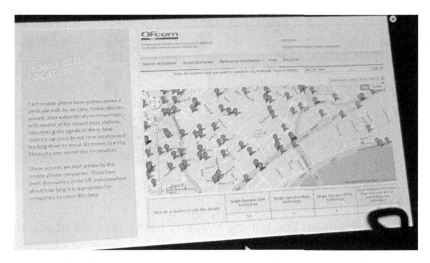

It states:

Each mobile phone base station serves a particular cell. As we carry mobile devices around, they automatically communicate with several of the closest base stations. Interpreting the signals to these base stations can provide real time location and tracking to about 50 meters in a city. Networks also record this information.

These records are kept private by the mobile phone companies. There have been discussions in the UK and elsewhere about how long it is appropriate for companies to retain this data.

It states:

The GPS (Global Positioning System), uses a network of around 30 satellites. Each transmitting precise position and time information. A GPS receiver picks up signals from three or more of these satellites and uses the time taken for the signal to reach the device from the sad lives to work at its precise position on earth.

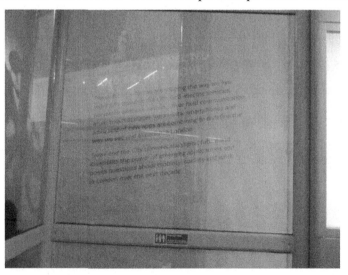

As you enter the exhibit there's a sign that says **Smart Connected and On the Move:**

Powerful new forces our shaping the way we live, work and travel in the city. GPS, electric vehicles, pervasive wireless, sensing, near field communication, multi touch surfaces, open data, smartphones and a Blizzard of new apps are combining to redefine the way we see and experience London.

Since in the city unravels the digital future and illustrates the power of emerging applications and poses questions about mobility, society and work in London over the next decade.

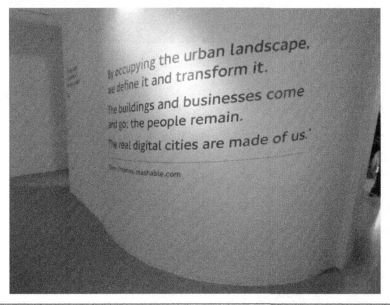

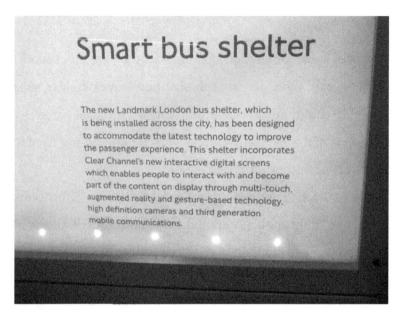

In other words, we will be watching you at the bus shelters.

Notice that data is in the TRANSPORTATION MUSEUM! Why? It's because data travels across the information highway through https, which means hyper-text transfer protocol; or if it is https it means hyper-text transfer protocol secured. Data travels across fiber optics, cable, power lines, satellite beams, etc.

I saw these cameras all over London with microphones! Big Brother is not even the word for it!

London Transport Museum 2012

All of this was from 2012. God put me in the White House in 2019 to see it all coming together. I must show you this as we delve more into the Metaverse. The digital ID system. In Europe it's called **Next Generation EU**.

A billion people have no legal identity - but a new app plans to change that

- A billion people in the world have no legal identity.
- Without an ID they can't open a bank account, get a loan, or even vote.
- Now a tech entrepreneur has come up with an answer.
- Joseph Thompson's digital app allows people to prove and protect their identity.
- His company, AID:Tech, has also found a way to protect charity funds from corruption.

- A legal identity is not just about opening a bank account: access to healthcare and your right to vote may depend on it. But just under 1 billion people in the world can't prove who they are, according to the World Bank.

It's an issue that tech entrepreneur Joseph Thompson has found a way to tackle. His start-up AID:Tech has created a digital app that allows people without official documents to create a personal legal identity.

A UN goal

Ensuring everyone has a legal identity, including birth registration, by 2030 is one of the United Nations' Sustainable Development Goals (SDGs). It prompted the World Bank to launch its Identification for Development (ID4D) initiative in 2014.

The latest data from the Bank shows there are just over 987 million people in the world who have no legal identity, down from 1.5 billion in 2016. The majority live in low-income countries where almost 45% of women and 28% of men lack a legal ID.

For the almost 80 million people forced to flee their homes by war or persecution last year, the situation is even worse. Identity documents are often lost in the confusion and yet they can be vital to the success of their claim for refugee status.[9]

In this article he speaks about using a smartphone

---

[9] https://www.weforum.org/agenda/2020/11/legal-identity-id-app-aid-tech/

3
What is the Metaverse?

The Metaverse is the Luciferianism reality created for humans. It is a world of fake, synthetic, make-believe images.

> *In Hebrew, META means Death*
> *Death to the Verse? Death to the Bible?*

It is described as an alternate digital world that immerses you once you enter. The word immerse means same as you being baptized into the new reality. Think of how we immerse in water to pledge our loyalty to the one true God – Jesus. In the fake world, they want you to immerse your brain into the cesspool of wild imagination. However, let's look at how they officially describe this new world…

THE METAVERSE CAN BE DEFINED AS A SIMULATED DIGITAL ENVIRONMENT THAT USES AUGMENTED REALITY (AR), VIRTUAL REALITY (VR), AND BLOCKCHAIN, ALONG WITH CONCEPTS FROM SOCIAL MEDIA, TO CREATE SPACES FOR RICH USER INTERACTION MIMICKING THE REAL WORLD.[10]

---

[10] https://www.xrtoday.com/mixed-reality/metaverse-meaning/

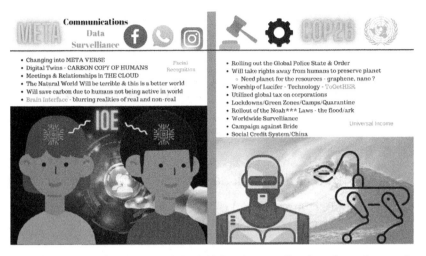

At COP26, and at DAVOS 2022, they talked a lot about the METAVERSE. So, this is here to stay. See my thoughts in graphics above.

In this world a digital you move from place to place unbounded by the laws and physics. This is the promise of the metaverse. Metaverse is the future of the internet.

Mark Zuckerberg recently announced his verse of the metaverse called META. He also owns the Oculus VR glasses. He describes the metaverse as:

"a Virtual environment where you can be present with people in digital spaces."

The metaverse was first described in a 1992 science fiction novel *Snow Crash*, that coined the term. In this fictional story, the metaverse is a parallel digital world where humans interact in avatar forms.

Metahumans

There is a new technology by Epic Games called Metahumans. It used to be extremely difficult to get really close to looking like humans. Now through the Metahumans program we can. We have sensors that drive the avatar's behavior. I can be in my studio with cameras and sensors on me and the other people will be doing the same thing but in the metaverse.[11]

In this world I can meet people in the Metaverse and present a really polished version of myself!

As you can tell by this description, they have invented ways to create digital twins of humans very realistically. Notice how the gentleman said that now he can present a perfect form of himself to the world. This is what is going to be so appealing to the Metaverse is the fact that people won't see the real you. You can look any way you want to and be anonymous if you like.

This all goes back to my theory of Trump and the Beast. Trump's world is like the Metaverse. It's very fake, synthetic, elite, carved up, hybrids, etc. They're too perfect. This world is like the Metaverse. It's not reality. Reality is that we age. We get wrinkles when we reach a certain age, etc. The fake world is a denial and a smack at God for bringing on the death process.

---

[11] https://youtu.be/rvGbE5Suf58 Metaverse: What the Future of Internet Could Look Like

Each day we live is another day headed towards death. Gravity takes over, etc.

Many of the men attached to Trump leave their wives of their youth and mothers of their children to be with better versions (in their mind) of women. They want the appearance of success. It's a spirit of pride and arrogance. It's like NAR – THEY want the top of every mountain. They can't stand to be a servant like Jesus – they must be the best.

Metahumans & Marvel Comics

In DC Comics' DC Universe, a metahuman is a human with superpowers. The term is roughly synonymous with both mutant and mutate in the Marvel Universe and posthuman in the Windstorm and Ultimate Marvel Universes. In DC Comics, the term is used loosely in most instances to refer to any human-like being with extranormal powers and abilities, either cosmic, mutant, science, mystic, skill or tech in nature. A significant portion of these are normal human beings born with a genetic variant called the "metagene",[1] which causes them to gain powers and abilities during freak accidents or times of intense psychological distress.[12]

This is amazing because when I wrote *The American Exposé* book, I talked about the connection of NAR and superpowers. Now that it's all said and done, I see the connection plain as day! They describe this phenomenon as Joel's Army rising. This is a group of elites who will rise up with supernatural powers in the last day and defeat the devil's army in the world and takeover for Christianity.

---

[12] https://en.wikipedia.org/wiki/Metahuman

Although I believe in miracles and the supernatural, I know the Bible does not support this end-time scenario.

It records it as we will suffer as Jesus suffered. Many will be martyred.

Telepresence

Eventually their goal is for everyone to be in this world and not in the real one. This is exchanging human interaction for the fake synthetic world (Beast world). On a podcast on the World Economic Forum website, a leader states, "Some people prefer the word telecommuting, but we prefer the word telepresence.

It indicates you are present without being there physically. This will change urban life in a couple of ways.

1. People will be going to the office less over the long term
2. Dramatically reduce business travel. A lot more business travel will be done tele-presently.

As we bounce back from the pandemic, we will see less service jobs. (manual labor). This will slow down the process of people going from gathering versus meeting online. We can all move online simultaneously. The norm has shifted. [13]

---

[13] https://soundcloud.com/world-economic-forum/did-covid-kill-our-cities?utm_source=www.weforum.org&utm_campaign=wtshare&utm_medium=widget&utm_content=https%253A%252F%252Fsoundcloud.com%252Fworld-economic-forum%252Fdid-covid-kill-our-cities

The goal is to push everyone into
the Beast World – The Ark.

Metaverse and the 4th Industrial Revolution

When I was in London in 2012, they hosted the Olympics and it was the Queen's Jubilee year. The Olympics featured in the opening ceremony a show about the evolution of the Industrial Revolutions. It looked like they were worshiping the internet. Was it coincidence that it was the Queen's Jubilee Year, the Transportation Museum did Sense in the City at the same time? I do not believe it was a coincidence.

Look at this picture I took from 2012 Olympics:

Notice the design on the bottom. Remember the spider design from earlier? The legs of the data reaching everywhere. This is what the 4th Industrial Revolution is – technology ruling the world – AI.

The **Fourth Industrial Revolution** represents a fundamental change in the way we live, work and relate to one another.

It is a new chapter in human development, enabled by extraordinary technology advances commensurate with those of the first, second and third **industrial** revolutions.

These advances are merging the physical, digital and biological worlds in ways that create both huge promise and potential peril. The speed, breadth and depth of this revolution is forcing us to rethink how countries develop, how organisations create value and even what it means to be human. The Fourth Industrial Revolution is about more than just technology-driven change; it is an opportunity to help everyone, including leaders, policy-makers and people from all income groups and nations, to harness converging technologies in order to create an inclusive, human-centred future. The real opportunity is to look beyond technology, and find ways to give the greatest number of people the ability to positively impact their families, organisations and communities.[14]

---

[14] https://www.weforum.org/focus/fourth-industrial-revolution

Being that they are partnering with the Climate Change agenda, it makes sense how they are causing people to enjoy the Metaverse better. Even today on the Superbowl commercials, there was one with Facebook showing how miserable this teddy bear was in the real world. He was able to escape into the Metaverse and be happy as a lark. It is like a Ready Player One scenario. That movie describes a terrible world and they escaped through the VR glasses.

Descriptions of the Metaverse:

By NAR – The Council of 13 Address about 2022 - The Technology Revolution – 12/20/21

We are in the midst of one of the greatest revolutions since the industrial revolution. This revolution will be in the "unseen spaces" of the metaverse and web 3. Over the next few decades, the use of artificial intelligence and augmented reality, using at this point technology such as Oculus, will drastically change the world as we know it. The introduction of robotics into our everyday lives will take place.

God will give His people new ideas on how to create jobs and be on the cutting edge of developing jobs that will result in the promised transfer of wealth.

Generation Z will experience a movement of holiness. They will be so fervent before God that it will provoke the generations before them to join in with their consecration.

New waves of technology will be used that will result in hundreds of thousands of genuine conversions through the use of social media, such as TikTok and other new innovative tools.

There are many new technological breakthroughs coming that will involve the metaverse and Web 3, as well as cryptocurrency. Believers will become students of such things, and God will begin to put Christians on the forerunning edge of these technologies.

There was an admonition not to demonize these new technologies. They are neutral in and of themselves. Even though there is potential to use them for evil, we need to understand how to use them for good for the gospel's sake. The possibilities of using augmented reality for things such as training for surgery and so forth are many. This technology revolution will produce a great decentralization of the way we have done things in the past. Many structures will experience a decentralization. It will be important to discern when God is causing the structures to decentralize as opposed to Satan trying to break up and scatter structures. This will involve the economies of nations as well. The way we buy and sell will dramatically change over the next few years on an even larger scale than it already has. God will raise up a young generation who are futurists or are very prophetic in their abilities to function in the world of cryptocurrency, and great wealth will be created for the kingdom of God.[15]

---

[15] https://www.charismanews.com/culture/87835-prophetic-word-for-2022-the-era-of-the-holy-spirit-and-the-year-of-upgrade

This is terrible beyond measure. God's people will be sucked into the Metaverse by these people. We must warn them.

Walmart is getting serious about the Metaverse

The company's recent trademark filings indicate plans for NFTs and cryptocurrencies – 01/16/22

The retail giant filed for several trademarks on December 30th, suggesting plans to start selling virtual goods, including electronics, toys, appliances, sporting equipment, apparel, home decor, and more, as noted by CNBC.

There's mention of offering customers a digital currency, as well as the opportunity to buy and sell NFTs. Meanwhile, another application details possible "physical fitness training services" and "classes in the field of health and nutrition" that could take place in augmented reality (AR) and virtual reality environments (VR) — the company made a separate filing for the use of its name and logo in VR and AR.

WALMART ALSO FILED TRADEMARKS FOR "VERSE TO HOME," "VERSE TO CURB," AND "VERSE TO STORE"

As pointed out by Bloomberg, Walmart also filed trademarks for the names "Verse to Home," "Verse to Curb," and "Verse to Store," a hint that Walmart may be preparing a virtual shopping experience (that hopefully doesn't look like the one created for the company in 2017).

The filings are publicly available on the US Patent and Trademark Office's site, some of which are listed under the name "Walmart Connect," the retailer's digital advertising endeavor. You can access the filings by searching for "Walmart" or "Walmart Connect" on the Trademark Electronic Search System (TESS).16

Metaverse, electric cars, brain tech: Take a look at how the future of technology will look like

CES tech show in Las Vegas closed its 2022 edition on Friday (January 7). Here are some major highlights from the event

ES 2022, the concept of metaverse took a centre stage. Metaverse is described as a network of 3D virtual worlds focused on social connection.

It can be understood as a hypothetical iteration of the Internet as a single, universal virtual world, which will be facilitated by the use of virtual and augmented reality headsets.

From gaming to auto tech, companies such as Hyundai, Shiftall, Owo have showcased tech that will unlock the metaverse.

How the technology will evolve in future? Will there be a possibility of mind control with the help of technology? Yes, it might be.

---

[16] https://www.theverge.com/2022/1/16/22887011/walmart-metaverse-nft-cryptocurrency

French startup Wisear is working on technology that detects the signals that zip between the brain and certain muscles, in order to use them to operate connected devices. [17]

The metaverse has been a hot topic of conversation recently, with Facebook and Microsoft both staking claims. But what is the metaverse? And when will it get here?

Author Neal Stephenson is credited with coining the term "metaverse" in his 1992 science fiction novel "Snow Crash," in which he envisioned lifelike avatars who met in realistic 3D buildings and other virtual reality environments.

Since then, various developments have made mileposts on the way toward a real metaverse, an online virtual world which incorporates augmented reality, virtual reality, 3D holographic avatars, video and other means of communication. As the metaverse expands, it will offer a hyper-real alternative world for you to coexist in.

Inklings of the metaverse already exist in online game universes such as Fortnite, Minecraft and Roblox. And the companies behind those games have ambitions to be part of the evolution of the metaverse.[18]

---

[17] https://www.wionews.com/photos/metaverse-electric-cars-brain-tech-take-a-look-at-how-the-future-of-technology-will-look-like-443374#mind-control-technology-443316

[18] https://www.usatoday.com/story/tech/2021/11/10/metaverse-what-is-it-explained-facebook-microsoft-meta-vr/6337635001/

What is the Metaverse Exactly? – Wired Magazine

Broadly speaking, the technologies that make up the metaverse can include virtual reality—characterized by persistent virtual worlds that continue to exist even when you're not playing—as well as augmented reality that combines aspects of the digital and physical worlds. However, it doesn't require that those spaces be exclusively accessed via VR or AR. A virtual world, like aspects of Fortnite that can be accessed through PCs, game consoles, and even phones, could be metaverse.

It also translates to a digital economy, where users can create, buy, and sell goods.

And, in the more idealistic visions of the metaverse, it's interoperable, allowing you to take virtual items like clothes or cars from one platform to another. In the real world, you can buy a shirt from the mall and then wear it to a movie theater. Right now, most platforms have virtual identities, avatars, and inventories that are tied to just one platform, but a metaverse might allow you to create a persona that you can take everywhere as easily as you can copy your profile picture from one social network to another.[19]

As you can see, it's the world-wide-web zoo! It's mixed with crypto currency and a whole new world. We already see many of the head leaders of NAR making money already on this world. Very sad.

---

[19] https://www.wired.com/story/what-is-the-metaverse/

4
METAVERSE & SOCIAL MEDIA

This is the perfect time to talk about Mark Zuckerberg. He is the creator of Facebook and now the leader of the Metaverse. He is redefining how social media is interacting with people. Let's review the history of social media:

Facebook is set to become a 'metaverse' company - what could that mean for society?

Facebook chief executive Mark Zuckerberg recently <u>announced</u> the tech giant will shift from being a social media company to becoming "a metaverse company", functioning in an "embodied internet" that blends real and virtual worlds more than ever before.

In South Korea, for example, a "<u>metaverse alliance</u>" is working to persuade companies and government to work together to develop an open national VR platform. A big part of this is finding ways to blend smartphones, 5G networks, augmented reality, virtual currencies and social networks to solve problems for society (and, more cynically, make profits).

The idea of a metaverse, by shifting even more of our lives onto a universal platform, extends this problem to a deeper level. It offers us limitless possibility to overcome the constraints of the physical world; yet in doing so, only replaces them with constraints imposed by what the metaverse will allow.[20]

Metaverse as the next major computing platform

The internet today is often the main entry point for millions of us to access information and services, communicate and socialize with each other, sell goods, and entertain ourselves. The metaverse is predicted to replicate this value proposition - with the main difference being that distinction between being offline and online will be much harder to delineate.

This could manifest itself in several ways, but many experts believe that "extended reality" (XR) – the combination of augmented, virtual and mixed reality – will play an important role. Central to the concept of the metaverse is the idea that virtual, 3D environments that are accessible and interactive in real time will become the transformative medium for social and business engagement. If they are to become practical, these environments will be dependent on widespread adoption of extended reality.[21]

01-04-22 - The metaverse is a second chance to right the wrongs of social media. Here's how

---

[20] https://www.weforum.org/agenda/2021/10/facebook-is-set-to-become-a-metaverse-company-what-could-that-mean-for-society
[21] https://www.weforum.org/agenda/2021/10/what-is-the-metaverse-why-care/

Where AR offers accessibility, extension, and functionality, gaming and VR sit at the other end of the spectrum, delving into the emotional and immersive. Luxury fashion brands have taken first steps in exploring what's possible. Balenciaga dipped into *Fortnite* by co-releasing a limited collection and an in-game cosmetic drop. This is an incredible opportunity to make inroads with a young audience that might not have the capital now, but will one day. Meanwhile, Burberry launched its first NFT collection last summer. These brands don't necessarily expect the end result to be a purchase; the bigger win is the chance to build a brand pathway, develop a relationship, and begin a more engaging, deeper dialogue with audiences.[22]

Moving into the metaverse

Facebook's name change may have bought mainstream attention to the possibilities of the metaverse, but the road is already being paved by many big names who first cut their teeth on social media.

Gary Vaynerchuk, CEO of VaynerMedia, identified the Internet as a land-grab opportunity and opened one of the first eCommerce platforms in the late 90s. He essentially grew with social media, becoming a hugely prolific and influential name within the industry, and has been investing in the Metaverse for the past two years,

---

[22] https://www.fastcompany.com/90710082/the-metaverse-is-a-second-chance-to-right-the-wrongs-of-social-media-heres-how

creating and developing Vee Friends, an NFT brand company, as well as other Web 3.0 initiatives.

Other early-adopters of social media, such as Social Chain co-founder, and youngest-ever investor on Dragon's Den, Steven Bartlett, has also begun investing in a number of Web 3.0 companies, while social media pioneer Cathal Berragan moved from Social Chain New York to a Web 3.0 business in London.

A good friend, Tom Osman, has since founded an incredible community in the Shiny Object Social Club following his sale of an ETH rock for 400 Ethereum ($1,326,280.00) at the time.

While these are just a handful of names, all are using their significant social media followings and the skills they learnt on those platforms to make the transition into this new space.[23]

Metaverse

What are the Five Laws of the Metaverse?

The Metaverse; "Web 3.0" the "Evolution of Digital" a "Successor State" to the internet, whatever it's being called, it's here. Uhive is the first social network to merge our physical reality with the digital world by following the Five Laws of the Metaverse, in the process aligning culture, communities, shopping, entertainment, and economies, a convergence known as the Social Metaverse.[24]

---

[23] http://elitebusinessmagazine.co.uk/sales-marketing/item/web-30-and-the-metaverse-is-this-the-future-of-social-media

[24] https://www.uhive.com/?gclid=CjwKCAiA9aKQBhBREiwAyGP5lcD8hDR6fmwOpuuTFo3kLiqU_7aXprLZ09KH99Ipwv7--Twp2byqbRoCbKkQAvD_BwE

Let's Look on Their Websites:

Facebook: (Meta)

The metaverse is the next evolution of social connection. Our company's vision is to help bring the metaverse to life, so we are changing our name to reflect our commitment to this future.

The metaverse will be social

3D spaces in the metaverse will let you socialize, learn, collaborate and play in ways that go beyond what we can imagine. Listen to Mark Zuckerberg share our vision for bringing the metaverse to life together.[25] Facebook is also Instagram.

Twitter:

These themes suggest that social intelligence has truly come into its own over the past year with numerous trends conspiring to drive awareness and adoption. Despite that, many organizations still consider social data a marketing-specific resource and undervalue its business impact. Sprout Social's recent Index survey highlighted this very point, reporting that 46% of respondents saw social data strictly as a marketing resource. Clearly, there's still work to be done and people to win over, however this shouldn't take away from the 54% who saw social data in a more strategic light.

---

[25] https://about.facebook.com/meta/

And after such a challenging year, why not see the glass as half full?[26]

YouTube: YOUTUBE APP

Phone

- Make sure you have YouTube installed on your device.
- Visit the Virtual Reality YouTube channel in your phone's YouTube app to find the best VR videos.
- Look for the icon in the lower right of a video to tell you it's VR.
- Once the video is playing, tap and drag the screen to look around...
- Or simply move your phone around to explore.

Desktop

- Visit the Virtual Reality YouTube channel in your phone's YouTube app to find the best VR videos.
- Look for the compass icon in the upper left of a video to tell you it's VR.
- Start playing the video.
- Use your mouse to click and drag the video to look around.[27]

---

[26] https://blog.twitter.com/en_us/topics/insights/2021/the-state-of-social-intelligence-2021-year-in-review

[27] https://vr.youtube.com/watch/

Dangers of Metaverse on Social Media

When Facebook changed their name to Meta, I prepared a video to warn of Facebook. The powers-that-be will take our data in the future and use it against us. I replayed my video today for church called *The Fiber for the Cyber*. This is a warning of the exposure coming to the church.

I also reported within past couple of weeks how the Council of 13 NAR leaders are telling their people that there will be an attack to the church this year of exposure. You know if they are warning people that we are on the cusp of this thing.

All of the major events in the Earth (Coronavirus, Great Reset, etc.), up until Meta was rolled out only laid the path for this new world. You can see how people will welcome this new fascinating world. We must be aware so we can prepare our families.

Jack Dorsey mocks Mark Zuckerberg's metaverse plan, saying it's dystopian

10-21-21 Twitter CEO Jack Dorsey has made fun of the "metaverse," a concept Facebook CEO Mark Zuckerberg has been pushing as the future of both Facebook and the internet at large.

The "metaverse" refers to a future version of the internet where, instead of accessing the web through laptops and phones, people use virtual-reality and augmented-reality devices to enter a virtual space.

Dorsey indicated late on Tuesday that he thought the idea was dystopian.[28]

Connected to Blockchain

As a church, we cannot participate in the Circular Economy's digital money such as crypto currencies and NFT's, etc. This is Satan's world and we cannot do this. According to Yahoo Sports, "The metaverse is basically what will come after the internet.

It's a virtual space where humans - tethered to the physical world - can operate using virtual and augmented reality-powered avatars and exist in both places, losing touch on what's real and what's not.

Some pop culture examples of metaverses include "Ready Player One" and "The Matrix."

The metaverse already existed in some forms within the gaming world, like in "Animal Crossing" and "Roblox." "Fortnite" creator Epic Games' CEO Tim Sweeney said in April after receiving a new funding round that it's grateful to investors "who support our visions for Epic and the Metaverse" and its work with "connected social experiences."

It also has associations with blockchain. The decentralized, digital asset could theoretically be used to pay for goods and services in the virtual universe.[29]

---

[28] https://www.businessinsider.com/facebook-metaverse-jack-dorsey-criticizes-as-dystopian-mark-zuckerberg-2021-10

[29] https://sports.yahoo.com/mark-zuckerberg-wants-expand-facebook-133610564.html

Tearing Down Old Order of Social Media

As a part of the Great Reset, they are tearing down the old order of social media to replace it with the Metaverse. The old social media used to be about human opinions and relationship. It was the real world connections – real names, etc.

The new order of social media will be the wild-wild-west in the Metaverse. They are going to do away with how we communicate. They are going to the climate control world – the circular economy. In this world, everything is ran by the human centered design – New Age.

This is a part of the build back better campaign. They are tearing down all of the old and bringing in the new.

According to Edward Snowden, "People do not talk to each other directly anymore. They talk to each other through social media. The platform designers have become more comfortable to tell people who they can hear from. The line of permissible speech has narrowed. The way these companies have handled complaints – Facebook especially." [30]

As Wired notes, many of the literary and cinematic depictions of metaverses include a quasi-apocalyptic, dystopian, or at least unlivable, real world. The metaverse, therefore, would provide a much-desired escape from whatever is so undesirable about reality. [31]

---

[30] Dangers of Facebook by Dr. June Knight – News Today Program -- https://youtu.be/toKsmjetQ6M

[31] https://www.businessinsider.com/what-is-metaverse-facebook-mark-zuckerberg-roblox-animal-crossing-2021-

Every human will be a policeman. They want have to worry about policeman because the humans will be that.

Brain Interface

MARK ZUCKERBERG WANTS TO READ YOUR HUMAN BRAIN

Facebook is bankrolling research into technology intended to read peoples' thoughts.

JULY 31, 2019

According to Vanity Fair, "Facebook on Wednesday announced that it has been bankrolling research into developing technology intended to read peoples' thoughts. The research, outlined by University of California San Francisco scientists in a paper, involved affixing electrodes to the brains of human volunteers, asking them questions, and attempting to determine what they are about to say by analyzing their brain activity.

Facebook and the researchers suggested the technology could be useful for "patients who cannot communicate," but the tech giant also described ways the brain-computer interface could be used by consumers. "Imagine a world where all the knowledge, fun, and utility of today's smartphones were instantly accessible and completely hands-free," the company wrote in a blog post.

8#:~:text=The%20metaverse%2C%20therefore%2C%20would%20provide,away%20from%20physical%20human%20interaction.

"Where you could spend quality time with the people who matter most in your life, whenever you want, no matter where in the world you happen to be. And where you could connect with others in a meaningful way, regardless of external distractions, geographic constraints, and even physical disabilities and limitations...That's the future we believe in."

Whether you view that future as thrilling or terrifying depends on how much you trust Mark Zuckerberg, who has faced a deluge of criticism for his company's handling of user privacy—including, recently, from Chris Hughes, his former roommate and collaborator who has publicly accused the Facebook co-founder of pursuing "domination" without thought to the consequences. "He's human," Hughes wrote of Zuckerberg in a bombshell New York Times op-ed last March calling for regulators to break up Facebook. "But it's his very humanity that makes his unchecked power so problematic." Reports have since emerged that Hughes is meeting with regulators in Washington to prod them into taking action against the company he helped create.[32]

Brain-reading tech is coming. The law is not ready to protect us.

---

[32] https://www.vanityfair.com/news/2019/07/mark-zuckerberg-facebook-brain-computer-interface

In the era of neurocapitalism, your brain needs new rights.

Over the past few months, Facebook and Elon Musk's Neuralink have announced that they're building tech to read your mind — literally.

Mark Zuckerberg's company is funding research on brain-computer interfaces (BCIs) that can **pick up thoughts directly from your neurons and translate them into words**. The researchers say they've already built an algorithm that can decode words from brain activity in real time.

And Musk's company has created **flexible "threads" that can be implanted into a brain** and could one day allow you to control your smartphone or computer with just your thoughts. Musk wants to start testing in humans by the end of next year.

Other companies such as Kernel, Emotiv, and Neurosky are also working on brain tech. They say they're building it for ethical purposes, like helping people with paralysis control their devices.[33]

Facebook: Here comes the AI of the Metaverse

To operate in augmented and virtual reality, Facebook believes artificial intelligence will need to develop an "egocentric perspective."

---

[33] https://www.vox.com/2019/8/30/20835137/facebook-zuckerberg-elon-musk-brain-mind-reading-neuroethics

To that end, the company on Thursday announced **Ego4D**, a data set of 2,792 hours of first-person video, and a set of benchmark tests for neural nets, designed to encourage the development of AI that is savvier about what it's like to move through virtual worlds from a first-person perspective.

The project is a collaboration between Facebook Reality Labs and scholars from 13 research institutions, including academic institutions and research labs. The details are laid out in a paper lead-authored by Facebook's Kristen Grauman, "Ego4D: Around the World in 2.8K Hours of Egocentric Video."

Grauman is a scientist with the company's Facebook AI Research unit. Her background as a professor at UT Austin has been focused on computer vision and machine learning in related topics.

The idea is that the data set will propel researchers to develop neural nets that excel at performing tasks from a first-person perspective -- in the same way that big datasets such as ImageNet propelled existing AI programs from a "spectator" perspective.

The point of egocentric perception is to try to fix the problems a neural network has with basic tasks, such as image recognition when the point of view of an image shifts from third-person to first-person, said Facebook. [34]

I encourage you to do more research about this Bride.

---

[34] https://www.zdnet.com/article/facebook-here-comes-the-ai-of-the-metaverse/

It all boils down to this picture – the final mark – the Digital ID where you will not be able to do anything without participating in this world:

35

As you look at this chart, it shows you how everything is connected. Remember:

- Internet of Things (IoT)
- Internet of Everything (IoE)
- Internet of DNA (IoDNA)
- Internet of Bodies (IoB)
- Internet of Medical Things (IoMT)
- Internet of Underwater Things (IoUT)

Interesting fact:

The fact that we route internet traffic through the ocean — amidst deep-sea creatures and hydrothermal vents — runs counter to most people's imaginings of the internet.

---

[35] https://www.weforum.org/agenda/2020/11/legal-identity-id-app-aid-tech/

Didn't we develop satellites and Wi-Fi to transmit signals through the air? Haven't we moved to the cloud? Undersea cable systems sound like a thing of the past.

The reality is that the cloud is actually under the ocean. Even though they might seem behind the times, fiber optic cables are actually state-of-the-art global communications technologies. Since they use light to encode information and remain unfettered by weather, cables carry data faster and cheaper than satellites. These systems are not going to be replaced by aerial communications any time soon.

The miles and miles of cables, which are roughly the size of a garden hose, carry internet traffic at the speed of light. They can carry so much traffic that fewer than 300 cable systems transport almost all internet traffic around the world.[36]

------

[36] https://medium.com/intuition/there-is-no-cloud-internet-is-under-the-ocean-d1af81d5b720

Dr. June Dawn Knight

5
METAVERSE & BEAST

In this chapter we are going to talk about the government, United Nations, businesses and the church's role in the Metaverse. This is a worldwide agenda. They are all involved.

<u>NOTES FROM DAVOS 2022</u>

KFB - *Head of d & Machine Learning WEF*

- # 16 other projects under AI to

- # Leap frogging using AI

IT - Tech Editor - *The Straits Times - Hostess from Singapore*

UN - Impact on COVID using AI going Forward

Transcript:

Good morning, thank you, Kay. Good morning and welcome to our panel on shaping the future of artificial intelligence, **IT, editor of the straits times**, a national daily newspaper in Singapore. And I'm your moderator today.

And we hope to have a conversation on the impact and the effect of the COVID pandemic on AI and its governance and how AI can be used going forward.

We saw AI's news accelerate as nations try flatten the COVID-19 infection curve even before AI rules and norms weren't yet in place. Many of these users required citizen to see forego their civil liberties and data protection rights. From robots that detect population movements and social gatherings in China, to aggressive tracing of the close contacts of the COVID patients using mobile location data in Israel and also credit card payments and facial data in South Korea, AI's use was nothing short of intrusive. When privacy is curtailed, it is important to revisit some of the government's gaffs and attempt to block them. Failing to do so will have a long-term impact on public health and privacy policies. Also, the social contracts between our Governments and the citizens in industries involving the use of predictive algorithms may also need to be redrawn, hopefully after some robust discussions on AI ethics to maintain public trust in AI's use over the long-term. In fact, some say that these conversations are overdue, so at this juncture, I would like to introduce our distinguished panel to talk about how AI can be used responsibly and how everyone can shape the future to ensure that AI technology benefits everyone.

I would like to introduce VD, President at the Patrick J. McGovern foundation, a tech change maker to use AI solutions to create an equitable future for all. Second we have MB, he's the CEO of Appen, a publicly traded company in Australia, and human annotated data set expert for training machines for machine-learning algorithms, and specifically Appen used tech and audio to improve AI systems.

They know we have HM, an ethicist at DataRobot, a Massachusetts-based company, implementing data usage for retail to healthcare, from antimony laundering, reducing false positives to laundry laundering, and reducing patient readmission rates.

And lastly, JM, who works in the White House with a focus on Technology and National Security. He is the deputy assistant to the President for Technology and National Security, a new role he has taken on. Each speaker will have a chance to provide their perspectives on the topic, during which the audience can submit questions using the chat function. We will have a Q&A session later on to address as many of these questions as possible, so do ensure that your questions are concise and relevant to the topic. So now we will invite Vilas to offer a perspective on philanthropy to -- how important is it for governments to have a strange AI policy and how can philanthropy put us on the road to supporting all of society.

20:53:58 VD President Patrick J. McGovern Foundation

Vie Irene, the World Economic Forum has taken great leadership on these questions, and I'm the President of a civil society organisation, The Patrick J. McGovern Foundation. And two observations. I've spent most of my life as a technologist and a human rights advocate. And I have to share just how optimistic I am about the power of technology to make the human experience better.

We're seeing it by the day in increasing agricultural yields and increasing access to education, finding new ways to express ourselves and form new connections, but in the context of that very positive observation, I have to make the second, which is I feel like we're very quickly tagging onto a Navy, of a three-sided stool, where technology companies innovate, governments regulate, and third, where We, the People become consumers rather than becoming cocreators. Now, coming into civil society and to your question, Irene, it's not so much that any one of those single characterizations are wrong -- but I would say they are -- but what's broken down is a social compact, one that doesn't put technology in the center, but rather one that puts individual and collective interests at the centre of the model. I think if we can get to the place where governments move first to understand their citizens needs and trying to increase innovation in tools that lead to a better future, where technology companies treat participants as part of the design of the technology and see where individuals have a voice through civil society, that can lead to a fundamental new social compact for the AI age. So, I'm excited for the large of the global AI action alliance, one of the core tenets of this programme is to bring actors together in one inclusive environment where the question can go from how we build responsible and ethical AI, to what does an ethical society look like when AI allows for entirely new form of economic and social values. I'm excited to explorer those topics with you, the pandemic as highlighted the opportunity to take that model that I'm describing and apply it at s scale.

Private Sector - MB - CEO Appen

20:56:31

IT: Thank you, violence, so consumers should be treated as a stakeholder in the development of AI, rather than the outcome.

So that's a good thought. So, let's hear from the private sector. Mark, as an executive of a layered in a company that is involved -- what is your goal for training AI, and what steps can companies do to get things right from the start. And if data is the starting point for training machines what, are the important considerations to data sets.

MB: Thank you, Irene, and thank you everybody. It's a pleasure to be here. It's a pleasure to be part of the conversation at the forum. Data is a really important consideration, and there's a few things that we look at to make sure that we're sourcing our and providing data responsibly. So, in short, the data becomes the AI. So, if you have, for example, a biased data set, you're going to get a biased AI outcome. There's three areas that we look at when we look at data, and this builds on Vilas' comments about the role of cure. The first is data privacy. We -- the role of the consumer -- we make sure that we're consistent with all of the legislations around data privacy. That we seek consent for the at that time that we collect from people, etc. and so it's important, that we maintain those data that we collect, we maintain the security and the privacy of those throughout the use of that data. The second area is data bias.

Which is a topic that many people are familiar with in AI, quite simply, if you're trying to build a speech recognition product that works for all people, you need to collect data that is representative of all people, for example, representative tones of voice, representative accents. For example, if you have a data set exclusively of male voice, it's not going to work, the resulting AI is not going to work as well for female voices. So it's important to have an unbiased data set. The other area, which is an area that gets some press, but perhaps not as much, is around the ethical sourcing of data, and this is not just a privacy issue, but the treatment of the people that prepare the attachment we rely on a global crowd of over a million people to collect and label the data, and we have developed over time our own crowd of ethics that making sure that we're paying people correctly, being inclusive, that we're communicating our will to the crowd, etc. And now, there are some legislations in this area, as we know, there's things like GDPR for data privacy, ISO standards 27,001 for security and protection of data, there are modern slavery legislations that ensure that people in every part of the value chain are treated fairly. But there are also some challenges, to Vilas' point about the role of the consumer, there's a certain tension in that first of all data privacy legislation -- it varies by jurisdiction. Jurisdictions with lax data privacy that allow random data harvesting, ironically are going to build better AI because they have that, so there's that tension in privacy and the AI outcome. The other area is that is also a challenge is in the area of data bias.

So, to go back to the previous example, on voice tone, in order to round down a data set, for example, if you have a lot of male voice tones, you have to discriminate in your data collection and collect female voice tones only, and that becomes a bit of a challenge when we're trying to do everything fairly and openly. So, the completeness and the fairness of the data sets are important contributor to AI. We do a number of things at Appen that support those things, but there's work to go done in this area because it's very inconsistent across the globe and across jurisdictions.

JM - *Deputy Assistant to the President for Science & Technology - WH*
21:00:47

IT: Thank you, Mark. Now, we turn to Jason for government voice. You serve as commissioner on the Pentagon national house security commissions on artificial intelligence, and the commissions recommended last month several changes to the national AI policy that you now oversee at the White House.

21:01:09

So, from your perspective, how can AI be used responsibly? Perhaps with specific measures where possible, and also addressing the questions we ask, how important is it for governments to have a strong AI and data science policy or strategy.

JM: Thanks, Irene. It's about pleasure to be here with so many friends, who I know are in the audience and on this panel.

And just as the history of AI is one of international collaboration, so will be its future.

21:01:46

So, there's two parts of AI where I think government need to be especially mindful, and where the international community needs to be especially active. And that's first advancing privacy preserving AI, and second, advancing safe AI. On privacy, our global approach needs a revamp. In a recent survey of American attitudes towards AI, respondents' number 1 concern was that AI-assisted surveillance would violate privacy and civil liberties. Europe has one of the most comprehensive regulations in the world, but it has more or less the same technical vulnerability to say privacy as existed before (. There is privacy-preserving AI such that can achieve both our privacy goals as well as the performance goals. And further off we have the prospect of fully homomorphic encryption, so that we can protect data while at rest, in motion, and during processing. So, one goal for us both in the United States, but also, I think internationally, is to ensure that our national and international standards for AI, such as those that are being developed under ISOS342 are compatible with privacy-protecting methods. And I think we should work collaboratively in the international research community to refine those privacy-preserving methods, so that we can achieve our privacy goals and performance goals simultaneously. Safety is another area both for national attention and for international collaboration. We don't yet have design principles to provide safety guarantees in AI.

The United States supports both the OECD AI principles, and the work ever the global partnership on AI, both of which emphasize the robust and secure systems, and that are safe, but we need ways to reliably measure those processors. We don't have those methods currently. We also need to work towards technical standards, and measurement approaches to make safe AI systems, and I think one opportunity for international collaboration is a shared tech bed in which to test methods against known failure modes and to develop new methods for measuring robustness under a variety of conditions. So, I look forward to the discussion of these, and finding ways to cooperate so that we achieve progress on both.

IT: Thanks, Jason. On the point you mentioned about international cooperation, this is a point which I'll ask Haniyeh as well later on, social norms vary from place to place, CCTV and robot surveillance may be accepted in one place and rejected in another, and there is no one-size-fits-all solution, how do you ensure that this cooperation achieve the objectives that will be beneficial to all the stakeholders as part of these cooperation he was the? Jason, perhaps you could take the question first, and then later I'll turn to Haniyeh to talk about some of the more overarching universal principles that may apply and work.

JM: Yeah. I mean, I think that we have birthed a variety of principal that almost every AI developer in almost every country on the planet are going to agree are important, or that we should aspire to have our AI systems.

21:05:33

Robustness, ensuring that a system operates within safe limit --
assurance so, to establish that it can be analyzed and understood easily
by human operators. Specification, ensuring that it's align winning the
system designer's intentions.

Those are all properties that not only developers aspire to, but also
that citizen and see policymakers aspire to. So, I think there's actually
enormous room for agreement on many of these principles.

IT: Okay, cool.   Haniyeh, would you like to provide your
perspective from how some companies have operationalized some of
these universal ethical principles in their implications. >>

HM: *Global AI Ethicist DataRobot*

Sure, absolutely. Yeah, it's kind of like following up on what Jason
was saying, there are some processes that everyone can agree on. The
way to collect the data. There should be consent around it. You know,
as Mark was talking about, about the bias that can appear in the dark
how we can address that. And -- in the data -- and putting in
protections in place for the users to be able to understand and
recognise the problem, so they would be able to take action based on
that. And, kind of understanding, as you mentioned, these norms can
be different. What we define as a protected class in the US may not
apply to other countries. So, it's not understanding what's the main
goal and objectives for us, whether it's about fairness, for example:
What is it that we are trying to achieve. I think we can have a common
ground in that area and work on the details for each region separately.

IT: Right. On some of the technical metrics mentioned earlier - - Jason touched on federated learning, and ensuring that data at rest and data in process is encrypted, there are also a couple of other measures, like being transparent about what data is used to train algorithms, and revealing if algorithms can generate consistent results across a diverse range of people, and the margin of error, you know, and revealing what the margin of error is, it will go a long way to build trust in AI, but A practitioners, are they to that go today? Is it lacking?

VD - *Patrick J. McGovern Foundation*

Are there areas which we can improve on? Anybody can take this question. I like the question -- I think you're right that AI practitioners are beginning to have these conversations about how we apply the technical elements to go back to the sourcing of detachment, but I might just suggest we take one step further back. You asked a question about how regional and national differences perceive acceptable norms should define our ways we deploy AI. And I would suggest there is a moment to reconceptualize exactly what the interests of the individual are, in a data-driven economy. We talk about privacy and making sure that the data is representative, but we never go down to asking what are an individual's real interests in their data, and how do we conceptualize a AI process that recognises that individuals might have more rights in data that they use, not just in privacy, but being able to control on how the data is used, and being able to vote on how the data is used by AI practitioners. We need a conversation that starts with the interests and vulnerabilities of the model and then translates into how we build a responsible AI framework that integrates those interests. That conversation allows us to step out of the national frameworks that we're currently using, and even as we think about international cooperation to start again from a core conception of where the individual sits in the framework.

IT: Vilas, since you're on the topic, there is a question that just came in from the audience on your points early on: How can we use open-source solutions to quickly scale the infrastructure needed for government and citizens to play a more meaningful role in AI Joseph sight. Do you want to take that?

VD: Yeah, I love that question, and goes to something we talk about quite a bit, we talk about data as innovation, and wing we need to move from a world where the aggregation and collection of data is not the rules of the game but the starting point and the data infrastructure and how we apply analytics on it, this is important for open source community because most of the tools that we're using, perceptible in the nonprofit sector as we see companies trying to aggregate halted records for individuals who are in health systems, allows us to say let's not take tools off the shelf and try to fix them to they approach our challenges, but let's build entirely new mechanisms for managing things like electronic health records, for applying geospatial information on how we look at agricultural needs, those tools are created today, but what's missing is the framework to allow those tools to interact with the testimonies of social sector organisations.

IT: Going back to data and collection. The academic community, an idea from them is to allow people to own and price and sell their personal data, the idea is to share the profit from AI use, and companies benefit from using personal data, health data, intersequence, facial features, and location and voice patterns to train AI systems. What are your thoughts on this, MB? Do you think it's feasible?

MB: So, we've always remunerated the people that we collect the data from. So, if we ask somebody to record their voice, we pay them for it. If we ask people to label data, we pay them for it. So, to Vilas' point, what's the interest of the individual? A crude interest might be, hey, if we give you some money, will you let us use your voice in this particular product. There are probably more sophisticated ways of going about it, and we also get the person's consent to use the data in that way. It's an interesting thought, Irene, to open it up, because there's a lot of data being created as we sit here and speak. We're creating data.

So, should we benefit from the creation of the data? Should the WEF? Should Zoom? Who kind of --quote, unquote-- owns the data is pretty tricky, but I think the, certainly, creating the data is not always the problem. It's getting into a format that's usable, it's get filtering and parsing out data that may not be helpful, so there's sort of two steps in the chain -- there's the people that create the data and the people that prepare the data, and from where we come from, we make sure that we remunerate people. And I know all data that's used in AI, it is half ??(can't decipher) without knowing it. But our role is to make sure that people who do that work get reward for that work and that ownership.

IT: Thank you Mark. This question for Jason, what are the principles upon which governments can build a regulatory framework that protects human beings from the detrimental impact of AI while not preventing responsible AI innovation.

JM: Yeah. I really like the OECD principles -- positivity, fairness, transparency, robustness, accountability. And I think the OECD did a good job of explaining why each of those principles is necessary but individually collectively, though, I think it explains what we want our AI systems to achieve or aspire to. Now, translating those principles into specific instruments of governance, that's the most challenging part. That's something that we're working on at the White House, it's something that many governments across the world are thinking about, and it's something that the international organisations are also trying to think about collectively, which is I think going to be the most important work, is how we harmonize our efforts to embody these principles in law.

IT: Right. So, another question came in, and this, I think might be suitable for HM.

How might the private sector act as better balance tradeoffs between AI responsibility and their commitment to increasing shareholder value is an ethics question, true and true.

HM: Well, that is part of, when you're thinking about building an AI system. The first thing is what's the purpose of this system, how it's going to benefit, what's the positive and negative impact. If you minimize it. That also includes the fact that how we can hope that this AI system, help it to be kind of putting in place so that you can use it and brings value both for the private sector in terms of the profit that it has for them, but also how it can bring benefit to consumers, customers, users, of this system, that could be private citizens. So, in part of this process, at every stage, you can put guardrails in place to help ensure that this AI system would be ethical, that it aligns with the values that we have, and at the same time, it also has a tradeoff -- for example, sometimes you want to have an AI system that's more fair. That means that you may want to cut a little bit on your accuracy side. So, these are the type of things that, as part of these ethical processes, you would take into account in order to be able to create these AI systems that would be beneficial for everyone.

IT: Right. There's some who have argued for legislation as the language in integral framework are too general and they don't have the necessary specificity required for the principles to be operationalized. GJ, you mentioned briefly about putting some of the practises into law. Some have argued for legislation.

Is it too early to legislate some of these guidelines, could it create a false sense of security when the dangers of AI are in fact rampant? What are your views of legislation versus voluntary regulation.

JM: Yeah, I think the first step probably is coming up with technical standards that aim to be amenable to these principles. That is making sure that our systems are capable of expressing, our technical standards are capable of expressing these principles. We wouldn't want, for example, to set technical standards for AI that are incompatible with privacy-preserving methods like federated learning. So, I think as a first step, we should make sure that the technical standards we develop through SE42 and through other standards bodies are compatible with the principles that we think are especially essential, such as privacy. That in itself is insufficient. That is, I mean, even if we achieve those standards, we'll still need to do more, but I think that is a really practical first step that we can aspire to. And it's something we are working on. It's just that we need more voices at the table from the technical community to be recognising that these standards have enormous inertia. They'll stay with these systems for years. So, we need to bake in from the start a commitment to certain kinds of properties, such as privacy-preserving computing.

IT: Right. I think we have only time for one more question before I'll invite all the panelists to close with some comments. Okay. I think there's a lot of interest in expanded individual's rights to data and its usage in AI.

There's this question on international cooperation, and how it can be realistically promoted when national and political ideology such as those promoting government control versus individual rights are competing. Does anybody want to take this final question before we move to closing comments.

VD: That's quite a question for the few minutes we have left but let me suggest we have mechanisms through which we understand and normalize national interests around all kinds of things, treaties, and bilateral things, but the mechanism by which we come to a human consensus about the future is much more broad-based, and so I will suggest one that civil society can really play this role. That civil society across countries and geographic regions often can find commonalities of interest that are based on long-term and global goals. I think of things like reaching our climate goals. These are activities which despite all the unique national approaches have come together in some sort of global consortium of a goal, something that is universally acceptable. We can do the same things around an AI regime, but it requires voice beyond government actors, we have to empower and lift up those parts of the ecosystem as well. >>

IT: Any closing comments from the panelists before I hand the virtual mic over to Kay? Okay. Thank you so much. I think we're running really short on time, and I have kind of like -- I'm almost busting the time limit so, thank you, everybody, for your participation in the discussion today.

It's really, an accelerated use of AI to manage COVID and the global crisis has underscored the need to greater responsibility and transparency in and the development of the technology, many of the rules and norms which are yet in place should be discussed more robustly to ensure that AI's future is a successful one and is equitable and accessible to all in the community. Thank you, everybody, for your contributions, and I'll hand the virtual mic over to Kay, thank you, Kay. >>

KFB: Thank you, what a fantastic discussion.

FK: - *Deputy Exec Director Field Results & Innovation UNICEF*

Thank you, Irene, and thank you very much to our wonderful panelists tonight. It's now my great pleasure to introduce Mr. FK and invite him to give closing remarks for today's session. Mr. K is Deputy Executive Director, field results and innovation at UNICEF. He is also a member of the forum's global AI council, and has vociferously for more international cooperation for the development and deployment of responsible AI, especially as it relates to those who will be impacted most by the policies that we develop today -- the world's youth. Mr. K.

FK: Thank you, Kay. I think we've heard this evening the words accountability, transparency, and impartiality. These are fundamental elements of any ethical and human rights-based endeavor, especially in the field of AI. This has made today's discussion very, very fruitful. I'd like to put a child lens on all of this. If AI works for children, it works for everyone.

So, by applying the child lens to everything we do, we take care of generation AI. It's today's children: Those who use or are impacted by AI for their healthcare, their schooling, their communication, and eventually the jobs that they'll do. So, anything we do with respect to AI, we need to consider the children.

When AI works for children, it works for everyone. At UNICEF, we have a policy for the guidance of AI for children, which we've developed in partnership with the government (word) and it's encouraging to see that other governments are picking up on this and adopting this and putting this into their national policies. In May this year, we will be releasing the good governance for children's data manifesto, so please stay tuned for this. But what's also important to note is that the AI gap is exponential, as compared to the digital divide. We've heard the term digital public goods, and at UNICEF, we are cohosts of the digital public goods alliance in collaboration with Norway to make data, content, all open sources. We also heard the term of generation equality and in technology and innovation, of how governments and private sectors can work together and put all the pieces together to form policies that help with children and everything that they do. This is a once-in-a-generation opportunity to positively impacted children's lives everywhere. I consider it a privilege today to listen to the various perspectives being put forward, and for the various questions that were raised on the floor.

In closing, I think it's important that we all collaborate, we work together with government, we work together with entrepreneurs, both those established and aspiring.

I think we can work together to shape a brighter future for AI. And if I can close by saying, if AI works for children, it will work for everyone. Thank you, Kay.

KFB: Thank you very much, F. And what a wonderful and inspiring thing to say.

If it works for children, it works for everyone. And yet, you're absolutely right, that we need to be mindful of the people for whom we are thinking about, to we regulate, don't we regulate. What do companies do? What don't companies do? And so, thank you so much for those very inspiring remarks. It's liaison an absolute pleasure as well for us to be able to work with you, and Henrietta Fore at UNICEF, and many of your colleagues generally on shaping the technology to envisage excellent outcomes, and we have the smart toys initiative for which she will be a judge. We've also been working on UNICEF ton creating an AI youth council, because as Vilas so wonderfully put it, we need to really extend the number of people who are past our discussions on AI, and that should include young people from all over the world, and so we're really looking for one person, one child, from each country, to about 30 in that council. And that's just one of the very many things that we do on the AI platform at the World Economic Forum. So, as I extend, again, my huge thanks to our moderator, Irene, and our wonderful speakers, I honestly want to extend that thanks to you in the audience, and I hope that you very much enjoyed this session. I also invite you to be in touch with us for more information.

In the chat, you will find information about all the 16 projects that we have ongoing, as I, say, work with company and see governments to enable the development of AI responsibly, work with governments and companies, academics, and nonprofits around some of those high-risk issues such as the use of AI in human resources. And also, that work that F is talking about, and V is talking about: How do we use AI to get to a better place more quickly?

So, leapfrogging. Thinking about AI in chat box for healthcare, where doctors are not available to the majority of the population, or thinking about education with AI, and it's really about education that our smart toys award process tries to underpin -- what governance do we need for our children in the education? And so, with that, I'd again like to thank our speakers from DataRobot, Appen, The Patrick J. McGovern Foundation, and the Office of Science and Technology policy at the White House, and I invite you to have a look at those links, and also to follow more information on the global AI action alliance. We do have a number of sessions coming up, and so perhaps join us for one of those. The next one is on national AI strategies, at 2:30 in the morning. Central American time. And then after that, the topic that I talked about, chat box and healthcare, tomorrow morning, American time. So, thank you (end of session).

FINAL THOUGHTS

We do not want to be a part of the Metaverse. We know they are wanting the mind and the heart of the humans. Through the V, they are connecting the human body to the Internet of Everything (IoE) using the human centered design.

You are now at the center of this new world. They are gathering data off each mind, decisions, and movements.

It's like they are mice in a maze. They are watching, evaluating, experimenting, and making moves based on that data.

This is what President Trump is doing now with his new media! DANGER DANGER DANGER!

All I can do is warn. Please pray about how to go forward with this technology my brothers and sisters. Our souls are on the line.

HOW TO GET OUT OF THE METAVERSE

- First thing to do is to get off Facebook (data mining and cyber-attack coming)
- Get off all versions of Facebook – Instagram and WhatsAPP
- Get off Pinterest
- Get off Discord – it listens to everything around you! Terrible!
- Do NOT go into ANY of President Trump's media. Run for

your everlasting life! He is being used by the Devil against the Christians to lead them to the Beast (along with his cohorts – NAR)

- Be careful on any other social media. Do not go into any of the ones using bitcoins, NFT's, crypto currency, etc.
- Encourage your children and grandchildren that it is time now to get off virtual reality. Pull out of the matrix.
- Check your phone for the spyware like this:
  o Go to Settings
  o Then go to Health
  o Data at bottom says Data Access & Devices
  o Check at bottom where it says DEVICES, then click on your devices and see how they are keeping your health data. YOU CAN DELETE THIS.
    ▪ At bottom it says DELETE ALL DATA
    ▪ Delete it
- Turn off MEDICAL EXPOSURE
- Get rid of your Amazon Alexa's and all "assistance" out of the house – all listening devices
- Turn off Siri and other listening AI on your smart phones
- Know the time to get rid of cell phones and all electronics
- Slowly wean yourself off of the matrix.
- AI is here to stay, this is one of the main companies who leads it – DataRobot, "DataRobot was founded in 2012 to

democratize access to AI. Today, DataRobot is the AI Cloud leader, with a vision to deliver a unified platform for all users, all data types, and all environments to accelerate delivery of AI to production for every organization." [37]

- o It's not going away
- o It is taking over all industries

- o It will be measuring the mind of each human who enters the Metaverse
- Read your Bible and stay natural
  - o Don't bow to the pressure of the world
  - o Preserve your temple and keep it holy
- Pray

[37] https://www.datarobot.com/

ABOUT THE AUTHOR

We Are the Bride Ministries Founder

Dr. June Dawn Knight is a White House Correspondent, pastor, author, media specialist, mother and grandmother. Her heart is to serve her community. She has been in public service for the last 25 years. She spearheaded four organizations. The Middle Tennessee Jr. League Cheerleader's Association in which she unified four different counties and ten cities for cheerleading. MTJLCA still exists today. She also served as the president of the Steelworker's Union for the CMCSS Bus Drivers in 2004/2005. Then, she went to World Harvest Bible College in Columbus, Ohio. Following Bible College, she attended APSU from 2008 – 2012. During her time at APSU, she spearheaded three organizations on campus. Dr. June Dawn served student life and served on the Provost Committee for the students.

Dr. June Dawn graduated APSU in December 2012 with her master's Degree in Corporate Communication. She studied in London during Grad School under the top three global Public Relations/Advertising Firms in the world. During this time under the instruction of the University of Kentucky, she made a 100 in the class. She graduated with a 3.74 GPA. Dr. June Dawn had dreams of traveling the world for a major corporation, however, after graduation, God stopped her plans and called her back to the ministry.

Through the years Dr. June, as she is fondly referred to, has spearheaded multiple organizations that bring people together and give them a platform; many of which continue to function today. Additionally, Dr. June has served in multiple ministries all over the world working alongside visionaries to assist them in clearly defining, articulating and supporting implemental strategies that reflect and maximize the effectiveness of their Godly calling.

Currently as the CEO and president of WATB ministries, she has an astute ability to see through the deception that is unfolding in the world, along with an approach of reporting truth unlike any of our time. Her knowledge, experience and wit combined provide material that is godly, informative and life-changing for so many across the globe.

From London to the White House, Dr. June has been on an extraordinary journey to discover the heart of the spiritual condition of the country. The Lord intertwined her within ministries all over to give her a birds-eye view of ministry in today's culture. As the Lord sent her to the White House, remains a representative of the true church on a global level. She has the global picture of the church's situation and condition with the Lord.

Through the years of suffering, traveling and serving, Dr. June represented the Bride of Christ at the White House with truth and grace. The assignment there only lasted a year (the last year of America 2018-2019). Following this assignment, the Lord brought her back to Tennessee where she is now with her family.

From London to the White House. Now she writes books about what she has learned in order to help the Bride.

Dr. June's Education:

Bachelor's Degree in Public Relations at Austin Peay State University

Master's Degree in Corporate Communications at APSU. While in Graduate School at APSU, Dr. June studied in London (Winter 2011/2012) and studied under the top three global marketing/advertising/communication firms in the world. She wrote a 20-page research paper comparing how the United Kingdom markets a product versus the United States. Dr. June completed the class with a grade of 100! Following graduation, she turned that paper into her first book, *Mark of the Beast*.

- One year of studies at World Harvest Bible College
- Doctor of Theology at International Miracle Institute

Prior to this book, she has written 13 books. This is the fourth book of the *What the World?* Series. These books will help the Bride to understand the end-time events taking place and to prepare for Heaven.

KING HENRY VIII'S CHAIR!

KING HENRY VIII'S CASTLE

KING HENRY VIII'S CASTLE

HAMPTON COURT

KING HENRY VIII'S TREE

AT KING HENRY'S CASTLE

KING HENRY VIII'S CASTLE! SO COOL!

I trained under the top three global firms while i was in london. I had no idea where god was going to take me from there! look what the lord has done!

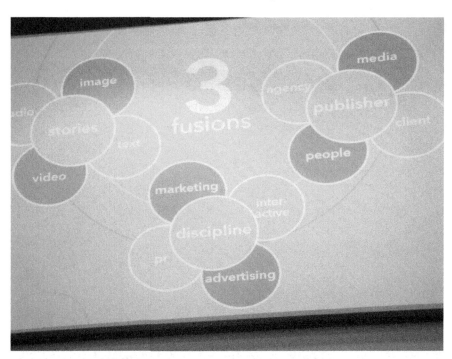

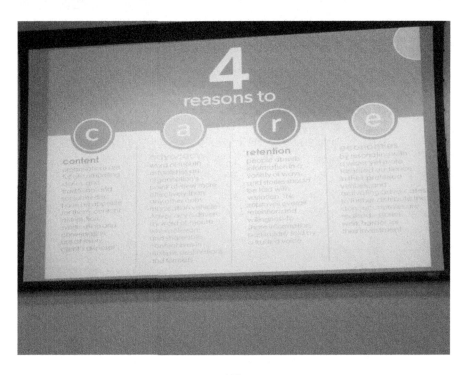

RIDING IN THE TUBE!

IN CHILDREN'S MUSEUM

THE TRANSPORTATION SYSTEM
CALLED "THE TUBE"

THIS WAS AN ADVERTISEMENT FROM DDB UK – WHERE I WAS TRAINED!

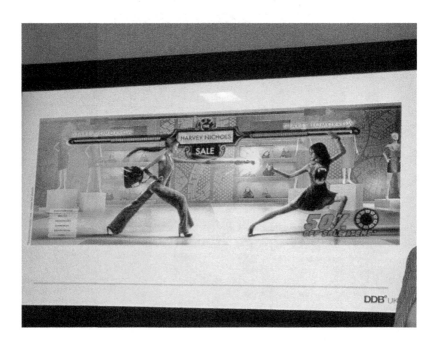

Made in the USA
Middletown, DE
21 February 2022

61546009R00086